EVANGELISM IN YOUR CHURCH SCHOOL

VINCIE ALESSI

Based on *Evangelism in the Sunday Church School*

by Kenneth L. Cober

Judson Press ® Valley Forge

EVANGELISM IN YOUR CHURCH SCHOOL

Library of Congress Cataloging in Publication Data

Alessi, Vincie.
 Evangelism in your church school.

 Based on Evangelism in the Sunday church school, by K. L. Cober.
 1. Evangelistic work. 2. Sunday-schools.
 I. Cober, Kenneth Lorne, 1902- Evangelism in the Sunday church school.
 II. Title.
 BV3793.A47   269'.2   77-16268
 ISBN 0-8170-0786-5

pp. 8, 22, H. Armstrong Roberts; p. 14, Toge Fujihira; p. 30, George A. Hammond; pp. 34, 36, Camerique; p. 54, Baptist Public Affairs

Introduction

"Help us with evangelism—evangelism in the church school!"
"Our church school isn't growing, and we don't know what to do about it!"
"Can you help us know how to be evangelistic in our church school? How do we go about it? What does it take?"
"Winning persons for Christ seems to be a difficult task. Can you give us some direction?"

These cries for "help" came from individual churches as well as the Counseling Committee for the Division of Church Education, which is part of the Board of Educational Ministries, American Baptist Churches. This book was inspired as a result of what appears to be a need of many local churches as expressed in the statements above. I have endeavored to respond to the expressed needs of local churches and of board members who represent churches in all geographical areas of our country.

Beginning with an attempt to define evangelism and then discussing some of the factors necessary to produce a climate conducive to evangelism, the book is addressed primarily to the church school teacher. However, some aspects of the book, such as chapter 2, "Getting into Action," focus on the administrators (boards/committees of Christian education, church school superintendents). Also, it has been suggested that the theme of the book—evangelism—is really applicable to every Christian, and perhaps the book should be recommended reading for all members of the congregation to help them with their personal commitments to winning persons to Christ. Questions at the end of each chapter will be helpful for individual thought and/or group discussion.

I would like to express my appreciation to Grant W. Hanson and Kenneth D. Blazier for their help and guidance as I prepared this manuscript and to Dr. Kenneth L. Cober for the suggestions and ideas drawn from his book *Evangelism in the Sunday Church School.*

It is my hope that teachers and administrators will find this book helpful as they endeavor to develop a program of evangelism in their church school and that they will have a productive experience in leading persons to an acceptance of Jesus Christ as Savior and Lord of their lives.

Vincie Alessi

Contents

1 Creating a Concern About Evangelism

"Go therefore and make disciples of all nations, baptizing them in the name of the Father and of the Son and of the Holy Spirit, teaching them to observe all that I have commanded you; and lo, I am with you always, to the close of the age."
(Matthew 28:19-20)

What Is Evangelism?

The above mandate by Jesus is at the heart of evangelism. It is the task of evangelism to

- bring all persons into living, active fellowship with God through Jesus Christ as divine Savior and Lord.
- gather all persons, through the regenerating power of the Holy Spirit, into the fellowship of the church.
- lead persons to express their Christian discipleship in every area of human life so that the kingdom of God may be realized.

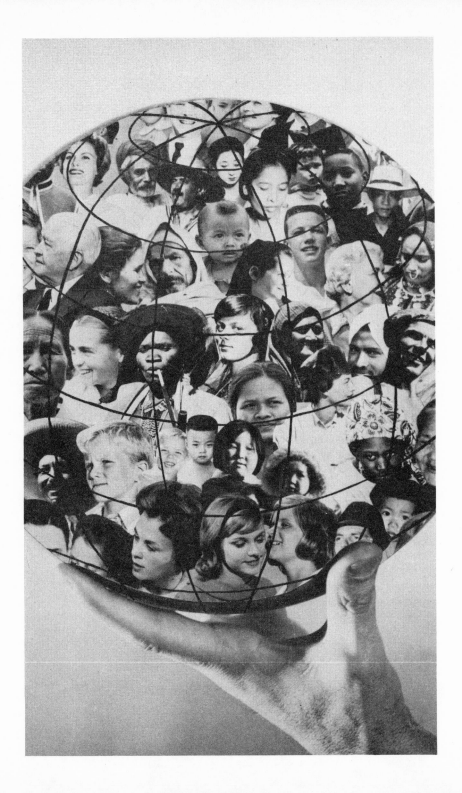

Evangelism is
- an attitude.
- a spirit.
- a living faith that finds expression in a continuous cooperative effort on the part of the Holy Spirit and humanity to bring individuals into a vital relationship with God and other persons through faith in Jesus Christ.

Evangelism results in
- a definite personal experience of salvation.
- a growing sensitivity to the social relevance of the gospel.
- a progressive building of Christlike character.

Evangelism seeks to bring persons into
- a complete harmony with the will of God.
- the fellowship of the church.
- involvement in the world as God's servants of reconciliation.

Evangelism is the task of the whole church,
- the minister,
- other staff members,
- board and committee members,
- *all other members* of the congregation.

Every Christian is called to share the faith and bear witness to the gospel. The experience of salvation places a claim on every Christian and on each local congregation to be responsible for the neighbor who has not acknowledged Jesus Christ as Savior and Lord.

> How are you and your church responding to Jesus' commandment to "Go . . . and make disciples. . . ."?

Probably everyone who reads this book will say, "Of course, we *are interested* in evangelism!" But "lip service" to this most important task of the church is not enough. *Talking* about evangelism produces little unless a spirit of concern has taken hold of a congregation. The "Good News" has to be communicated by the very life of the people. The message of the "Good News" is contagious and goes far beyond talk.

If you and your church are truly interested in developing a serious program of evangelism in the church school, there are certain factors which must be taken into account. Consider the comments in the remainder of this chapter as you contemplate "making disciples" for Christ and the church.

Atmosphere

Atmosphere is important! By "atmosphere" we mean the "feeling tone" of the church. Churches have different feeling tones:

- some are "formal," cold, closed to "outsiders."
- some are warm, happy places that communicate a spirit of community.

The atmosphere is not an artificial creation which can be produced on a moment's notice. It is, rather,

the product of a loving
concern for people.

This atmosphere might be characterized by a number of qualities:

- genuine interest in persons,
- spirit of acceptance,
- appreciation of differences,
- openness to dialogue,
- commitment to caring.

Consider some questions as you endeavor to determine what kind of "atmosphere" prevails in your church:

- Is your congregation generally optimistic, affirmative, and expectant, rather than gloomy and apathetic?
- Is there a predominant and pervasive spirit of joy abroad in your church as it goes about its work and worship?
- Is your church willing to change program schedules, traditions, and organizations, rather than try to change people to fit into "our way of doing things"?
- Does your church exhibit to any marked degree the ability to meet all the diverse needs of its own congregation and its community?

Priorities

Another important factor that must be dealt with when considering the evangelistic outreach of the church is the question of priorities.

The congregation must decide what is important to it. If evangelism does not have a place of primary importance in the mind of the congregation, little will be done about it. This is not a matter of "lip service," but rather a commitment of time, energy, and dollars! The priorities of the pastor and a few lay leaders may not be the priorities of the entire congregation. If a congregation is to develop a church-wide concern for evangelism, it is necessary that many people, not just a few, agree on priorities.

This concept is sometimes called "ownership." It means that people "buy into" something and make it their own. Does the sense of ownership (of an evangelistic program, ministry, goals) extend to most members of your congregation? Are the persons responsible for implementing these goals in ministry, service, outreach, program, and housekeeping responsibilities also involved in formulating the goals? If so, the prospects of your church launching a successful and active program of evangelism are excellent.

No church is ever going to develop a concern for evangelism unless there is ownership!

Purpose of the Church

Has your congregation prepared a written Statement of Purpose to use as a guide in its choices and ongoing life? Many churches have identified a New Testament definition of the purpose and role of their congregations in the world and are seeking to have their congregations be faithful to that definition and obedient to the call of the Lord where they are. Through such a Statement of Purpose, many churches have achieved a high degree of self-identity. They know who they are and their members reflect this knowledge.

Some churches have a Statement of Purpose as part of their Articles of Incorporation or Bylaws, but, unfortunately, it is seldom remembered.

An interesting experiment is to ask members of a group in a church to write out a statement of purpose for their church. Most groups find this a somewhat difficult, but rewarding, exercise. It usually happens that there is a considerable difference among the statements. At the same time, there is usually agreement about the fact that evangelism is part of the purpose of the church. Most churches accept the fact that they are called to bear witness to the "Good News" of Jesus Christ.

A congregation needs to take its stated purpose and recognize its responsibility for seeking to fulfill that purpose. A purpose which is stated but never implemented is in fact being denied.

Part of the growth and development of a congregation is the increasing self-consciousness of the reason for which it exists and of the mission to which it is called.

Being Intentional

Most results are planned, rather than accidental. Results in evangelism are no different.

Planning is related to priorities and the utilization of resources. It provides the process for responding with the available resources to the concerns which have been deemed the most important. It is a way of expressing responsible stewardship.

Planning is hard work, which requires time and effort. The suggestions in this book neither avoid hard work nor simply find the easy way. Kenneth D. Blazier in his book *Building an Effective Church School*[1] provides a chapter (chapter 6) on planning which will be helpful to a church developing a program of evangelism. *A Growing Church School,*[2] also by Mr. Blazier, will guide planners in their programs.

Evangelism in the church school does not just happen. Planning is a must! This book is dedicated to helping a congregation be intentional about developing the expression of its concern for evangelism in the church school.

[1] Kenneth D. Blazier, *Building an Effective Church School* (Valley Forge: Judson Press, 1976).
[2] Kenneth D. Blazier, *A Growing Church School* (Valley Forge: Judson Press, 1978).

For Thought and Discussion

1. How would you define evangelism?

2. Describe the "atmosphere" of your church. Is it conducive to evangelism? If not, what can you do to change the atmosphere to prepare the church school for an evangelistic thrust?

3. What is your understanding of "ownership"? Do you think it is essential to a program of evangelism? Why or why not?

4. What is the Statement of Purpose of your church? Does the program of your church reflect this Statement?

5. If your church does not have a stated purpose, consider developing one as a springboard for developing a program for action.

6. How would you go about planning a program of evangelism for your church school? List the steps you would take in developing such a program. (See *Building an Effective Church School* by Blazier, chapter 6.)

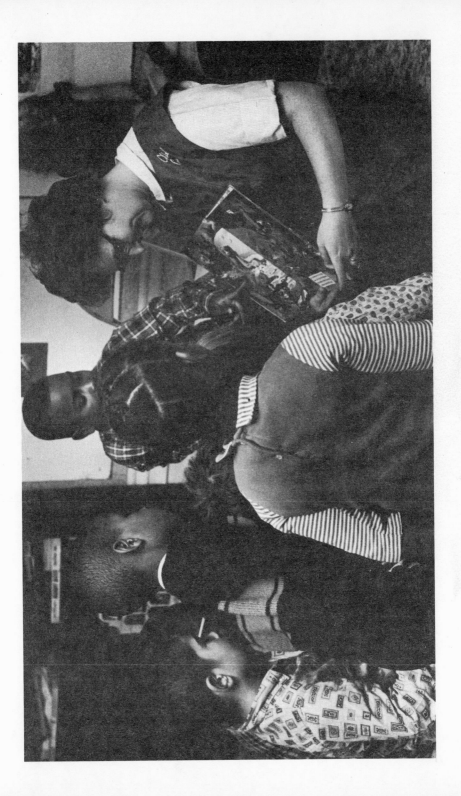

2 Getting into Action

Start with the Church

If the church school is to grow in strength and vitality,

- the pastor must be concerned and transmit his or her concern to others;
- the board of Christian education must meet and plan and work;
- the finance board or committee must undergird the program with adequate support.

But the church school is the responsibility of more than a few people; it is

every church member's job!

The church school is not a subsidiary of the church. It is

the church performing its
teaching ministry.

Therefore, the church must give its wholehearted support to the church school to make it an effective teaching and recruiting agency. This means that

church members, including adults, must participate

in the church school program either as leaders or students.

In a healthy, vital church program, the number of persons enrolled in the church school ought to exceed the number of members on the church roll. With this kind of support by the church, the church school becomes a dynamic force, an effective evangelistic agency. Add to the sizable core of church members the

- children who are too young to join the church,
- young people who have been recently recruited by the church school,
- adults who have not yet joined the church;

and you have a church school enrollment that is substantially larger than the church membership!

Until the church members show a strong concern for the church's teaching program, the church school will make a weak appeal to unreached persons in the community.

How can we get church members to take the church school seriously and participate in its program as students or leaders?

There must be an organized effort to recruit church school members by contacting candidates *personally* in their homes.

—Specially selected callers should canvass the constituency periodically and present the program of the church school.

—Callers should be trained for their work:

- informed about the church school program in order to answer questions intelligently,
- provided with suitable printed material to leave in the homes.

Provide for All Age Groups

If we accept the premises that

the church school is a school of the church

and that

every member of the church should participate in its sessions,

and if we believe that

the church school should serve as the organization
which provides all groups in the community with
Christian teaching;

then

the church has a compelling mandate to establish
classes and groups for persons of every age level—
from nursery to adults.

A gap in the organization indicates a group of persons for whom the
church is not providing adequate Christian teaching.

When a church school's organization is incomplete, more
persons may be lost than those in the age group which the gap
represents. For example, if there is no class for young married people,
attendance in the nursery is likely to suffer. If there are no classes or
groups for adults, then young people and even children will show less
interest and drop out of the program. Conversely, if a church school
adds several new adult classes or groups, a sizable number of new
students may be added to the younger departments, and the school
may double in attendance.

Start New Groups

* *The Nursery*

"What's the use of providing a program for infants?"
"What can infants learn in church school?"

The nursery is one of the most important departments in the
church school. Psychologists tell us that a college student in his or her
four years does not make proportionately a fraction of the progress
that a well-trained infant makes in his or her first two years. A child
learns more in his or her first twelve months than in any subsequent
period of twelve years.

"Twos" and "threes" and even the little "toddlers" can have
significant experiences in the nursery. Foundations of character and
religious experience can be established in the lives of these little ones
by the church—and more particularly by the home, when parents
receive guidance such as can be provided by the nursery teachers.
What a privilege to be the church school teacher who shares with the
parents the glorious opportunity of being the first to introduce a new
life to God revealed through Jesus Christ!

• *The Adult Department*

The adult department represents another age group which frequently is neglected and underorganized.

> "We have classes for them if they want to come.
> Surely there is no need to start new classes if we have
> room for them in the classes already organized."

This is faulty thinking. Every church school class is a magnet that attracts only certain people. It has peculiar characteristics, a "feel," a "climate," a "tone," which will appeal to persons who like what that particular class or group has to offer. Some people like:

• a men's class.
• a women's class.
• a "mixed" class.
• a large class.
• a small class.
• a class which studies a standard curriculum series.
• a class which selects elective courses.
• a class which has a teacher who takes the lead.
• a class whose teacher is merely a facilitator for discussion.
• a particular teacher.
• the students who make up the class.

In general, if a church school increases the number and variety of its adult classes, it will enroll a larger number of students.

Older, well-established classes frequently tend to become complacent; a newly organized class is likely to grow more rapidly and show more evangelistic concern.

Provide Qualified Teachers

Improvement in organization will have little value unless a church school has effective teachers. When naming the responsible leaders of the New Testament churches, the apostle Paul listed teachers along with evangelists, preachers, and apostles (1 Corinthians 12:28; Ephesians 4:11). In the church of our day, the work of every leader is important. But one can scarcely overestimate the significance of a consecrated, qualified church school teacher.

Because the teacher is so important, no one person should take on the sole responsibility of selecting the teaching staff. The church school staff should be chosen by a church-elected committee or board of Christian education. The committee or board should maintain a file of prospective teachers and make appointments only after it conducts a systematic study of all prospects, revealing the persons best qualified. Following are some qualifications which should particularly be kept in mind while evaluating the qualifications of prospective teachers:

- *Christian Experience*
  The teacher should
  - have a vital Christian faith.
  - be a committed Christian.
  - be a member of the church and actively support its program.
  - practice what he or she teaches.
  - make prayer an important part of his or her life.

- *Ability*
  The teacher should
  - have a teaching ability.
  - be adaptable to the age group assigned.
  - be able to communicate his or her faith.
  - have a winsome spirit.
  - show a cooperative attitude toward other leaders and toward the church school program.

- *Consecration*
  The teacher should
  - possess a sense of mission and urgency about the teaching task.
  - spend a *minimum* of two hours weekly in session preparation.
  - establish a rapport with the students and help them grow into the stature of the fullness of Christ.
  - have a concern for reaching the unreached.

- *Training*
  The teacher should
  - have training or experience.
  - be willing to take further training.
  - attend the church school workers' meetings.
  - read suggested books and magazines.
  - study the needs and experience of the age group taught.
  - grow on the job.

Unless the church school teacher possesses a goodly number of the foregoing qualities, no program of outreach and evangelism is likely to succeed. Teachers carelessly appointed who lack ability and consecration can lose whole classes from the church school and become stumbling blocks to students who are being led to consider God's plan of salvation.

Stress Evangelism in Curriculum

If teachers are to fulfill their evangelistic responsibility, they must use teaching materials which

- are based upon an evangelistic purpose.
- are unified around an objective that centers in the gospel message.
- provide experiences which will lead students into fellowship with God through an acceptance of Jesus Christ as Lord and Savior.
- take into account God's plan that life shall proceed according to his laws of growth.
- attempt to achieve their objectives progressively, building upon what has gone on before.
- help the students achieve all they can at their present stages in life.
- prepare students for future development and growth which come through lives surrendered to Jesus Christ.

For Thought and Discussion

1. Who is responsible for evangelism in the church school?

2. Is a nursery department important to a program of evangelism in the church school? Why or why not?

3. How many adult classes should a church school provide? What are the criteria for starting new classes?

4. What are the necessary qualifications for an effective church school teacher?

5. How important is curriculum in a program of evangelism in the church school? What characteristics should you look for when selecting curriculum?

3 Enlisting New Students

In the Gospel of Luke, chapter 15, we have three wonderful portraits of God—or, rather, the same portrait painted with different brush strokes. God is like

- a woman who loses a coin but sweeps and looks for it until she finds it,
- a shepherd who loses a sheep but never gives up the search until it is found,
- a father whose son journeys into a far country but who never closes the door against his return.

Matthew also records the parable of the lost sheep but gives it a different setting. Jesus was talking about the significance of children. He called a child and "put him in the midst of them"(Matthew 18:2). Then Matthew tells the parable much as Luke records it, except that the lost sheep is indicated to have been a child. He finishes the parable with the words of Jesus, "So it is not the will of my Father who is in heaven that one of these little ones should perish" (Matthew 18:14).

As long as one person—even a little child—is lost, God will follow that person with love and tenderness until that one is found and restored. If we share even a little of God's love and concern for the lost, no matter how many we have enrolled in our church schools we will still be moved to go out and win more.

Reaching the Unreached in the Community

We must do several things through the church school if we wish to reach the unreached in our community. We must—

Discover Who They Are

Scan the church's membership list for names of persons who do not attend church school.

Search for them in the membership rolls of the
- women's societies,
- men's fellowship,
- Boy and Girl Scouts,
- choirs,
- other church-related groups.

There may be other members in the families of these persons besides those actually enrolled in church-related organizations who also are good prospects.

Some churches register visitors in the morning worship service. Teachers should check the guest book or ask the pastor to provide information from the cards signed by visitors.

New arrivals in the community may be found by contacting the

- public utilities,
- schools,
- chamber of commerce,
- Welcome Wagon.

The students themselves can provide names and information of unreached persons with whom they associate in

- school,
- the office,
- the factory,
- community organizations.

Taking a religious census is a thorough and systematic method of finding the unreached.

Invite

The development of a "list" or the taking of a census is almost worthless unless the "discovered" persons are invited to attend.

We cannot overstress the importance of periodically conducting an organized and concerted effort to contact prospects.

Some things to remember when organizing a visitation program are:

- Visitors should be asked to participate well in advance so they can keep their calendars clear.
- The visitors may or may not be church school teachers. There are advantages to each.
- Conduct one or two training sessions to provide confidence.
- The training should furnish acquaintance with the total church school program so such questions may be answered intelligently.
- A descriptive piece of literature about the church school program would be helpful to the caller.
- Be persistent; allow for several calls to get results.

Conserve

It is vitally important to secure new students. But it is just as necessary to keep those now attending. A proper follow-up of absentees is fundamental in any well-organized church school. When a teacher looks at the absence record of a *former* church school student, he or she will no doubt find the following:

- first, an absentee;
- second, irregular in attendance;
- third, withdrawn.

It's as simple as that!

The time to follow up on an absent student is at once—within the day. The teacher is the logical one to do this. Let the student know that the teacher missed him or her, that the teacher enjoys having the student in the group. Make the student feel that his or her presence adds something which cannot be replaced and is sincerely wanted. If it will help, give the student a job to do.

Many churches follow a systematic plan for contacting absentees, such as:

1. When a student is absent the first time, the teacher sends a card with a personal message.
2. When a student is absent two consecutive sessions, the teacher contacts the student by telephone and discovers the

cause of absence; the teacher expresses concern and interest.
3. When a student is absent three consecutive sessions—a real danger signal—the teacher visits as soon as possible.
4. When a student is absent four consecutive sessions, the pastor is asked to make a personal visit. This may be the last chance to retain the student in the church school.

Each week, it is valuable for the teacher to notice and ask about the absent students. Expressing concern for absent students indicates to the class that the teacher considers regular attendance in the church school to be important.

Whatever else may be done to conserve students, it should be remembered that the most important factor is a week-by-week performance of effective teaching—a qualified teacher attending regularly with sessions faithfully prepared.

The Dual Role of the Teacher

The church school teacher must do more than teach religious truth. He or she must be a cultivator of Christian fellowship. The teacher must seek to reproduce within the class the kind of personal relationships and feelings of "group-ness" which characterizes the true church of Jesus Christ.

The effective teacher will

- demonstrate the characteristics of friendliness in spirit and action, in and outside of the class session;
- call in the home of each student at least once or twice a year;
- become acquainted with other members of each student's family and the environmental factors in the home which influence the student's life;
- encourage the use of take-home reading materials;
- call on students when they are ill or in some kind of trouble;
- gather helpful information about the students and remember them on birthdays and other anniversaries;
- congratulate students when they receive special honors or recognition in school or in the community;
- have good times with the students—help them plan parties, etc., and on occasion invite the students to his or her home.

"Aren't you asking a teacher to do a lot of work? Wouldn't the teacher have to give up some present activity?" Exactly so! The church school teacher who really does an effective job will devote considerable time to church school work. This teacher will take time to prepare well for weekly sessions. Obviously, this would mean giving up other things during these times. But the effective teacher will make this sacrifice because of his or her love for Christ and concern for people.

The Revised Standard Version of the Bible translates Philippians 2:5, "Have this mind among yourselves, which is yours in Christ Jesus." This translation makes clear that the word "yourselves" is plural in the original Greek and that the mind of Christ is to be made incarnate within groups of people and expressed in group relationships. Let the teacher first possess the mind of Christ within; then let her or him try to live and teach in such ways that the mind and spirit of Christ will permeate the class in all its relationships. In hearts and lives, students will come nearer to one another as they are brought closer to Christ. Warm, vital fellowships develop when teachers help students respond to the Master and share his purposes.

Utilize Student Initiative

Let us examine the ways some churches stimulate student initiative to build attendance and reach the unreached.

Rewards and Recognition

The giving of awards is one of the oldest techniques used by the church school to stimulate participation in the program. Christian educators generally frown upon this technique for these reasons:

1. It fosters the development of an "acquiring" nature contrary to the Christian values for which the church stands. It appeals to the student's selfishness. This is not in keeping with the spirit of self-giving and sacrifice taught by Christ.
2. It tends to develop a false sense of purpose. It misleads the student into thinking that mere attendance is the cardinal virtue, the "pearl of great price" sought by the church school. Thus, it becomes an end in itself, rather than the means to the accomplishment of other purposes.
3. Children can be harmed if the incentive for attaining perfect attendance leads them to attend when they are ill. They could also be the means of spreading their illness to others.
4. The time and money spent in maintaining a system of awards might better be used in strengthening the program by

providing better teaching materials and equipment.
5. An award system may serve as a substitute for a more vital program that emphasizes the development of an inner motivation related to the church's objectives.

Does this mean, then, that the church school is to make no recognition of the personal achievements of its members? No. We believe there is a valid distinction between the "winning of awards" and receiving a recognition of achievement. A program through which achievement is recognized can have value if the recognition meets the following conditions:

1. Highlights significant Christian values.
2. Does not exploit the individual by encouraging a selfish motivation.
3. Does not become an end in itself and dwarf the significance of the activity being recognized.
4. Does not promote competition and rivalry.
5. Is accompanied by an effort to develop an inner motivation and an appreciation of the activity for its own sake.

In other words, we will encourage regular attendance and the securing of new students because of the real significance of the church school experience and its ability to meet vital needs of persons.

Setting an Attendance Goal

The setting of an attendance goal is quite different from using rewards and recognition. It is good for a group to set a goal for new members and surpass its own record. As it is valuable for individuals to set goals for themselves, so it is equally valuable for groups to determine goals and attempt to reach them. In planning a program that makes use of an attendance goal, keep these principles in mind:

1. The goal should be high enough to provide incentive but not so high that it is unrealizable and causes discouragement.
2. The attendance goal should be part of a program which includes other goals which clearly indicate that mere attendance is not an end in itself.
3. The goal should be implemented with techniques for its realization; mere exhortation is not enough.
4. The students' efforts should be motivated by an appeal to the gospel and its implications.

For Thought and Discussion

1. How would you go about seeking names of prospective persons to reach for the church school?

2. How would you organize in order to make a systematic effort to reach the persons on your "prospective" list?

3. List some essential steps to remember when calling in the homes of prospective members for the church school.

4. Is it important to "conserve" the students presently on the church school rolls? How would you go about doing this?

5. What can the effective church school teacher do to cultivate Christian fellowship and a spirit of "group-ness" in his or her class?

6. How can you utilize student initiative?

7. Discuss the pros and cons of awards and recognitions as means of increasing church school attendance.

8. When is "recognition" valid in the church school?

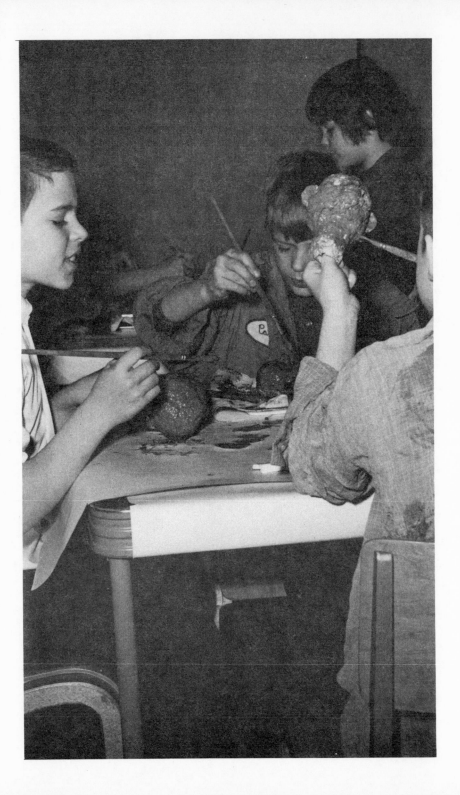

4 Providing Fellowship

The Importance of Fellowship

Our gospel began in the heart of God when he "so loved the world that he gave his only Son. . . ." We would be incapable of loving God had he not first loved us. It was because of his love that God sent his Son into the world that through Christ, God might be revealed to humanity and humanity reconciled to God.

Without love there would be no gospel and, hence, no church. If the church is to be the "body of Christ," then it must have the same quality of love which was revealed through Jesus.

Jesus repeatedly emphasized the significance of love:

> "A new commandment I give to you, that you love one another" (John 13:34).

> "This is my commandment, that you love one another" (John 15:12).

> "By this all men will know that you are my disciples, if you have love for one another" (John 13:35).

> "And this is his commandment, that we should believe in the name of his Son Jesus Christ and love

one another, just as he has commanded us" (1 John 3:23).

Never before was there a commandment like this—that we should form a fellowship whose chief business would be to love God and one another and then draw the whole world into this relationship of love.

The formal Sunday morning worship—except in the smallest churches—is too large to provide this fellowship with any adequate intensity, continuity, and concern for individuals. But in the informal gatherings of choir rehearsals, Bible classes, youth groups, men's groups, women's circles, church school classes, and other groups, fellowship with and interest in one another is natural and is one of the strong attractions to the group for most individuals.

The variety of these groups and their different purposes and interests appeal to persons of different aptitudes and interests. Groups greatly enrich the life of the church and enhance its power to win people to Christ.

A survey demonstrated a direct relationship between the number of conversions and the number of church school classes and other fellowship groups within a church. As the face-to-face fellowship groups in a church increase, the number of conversions and baptisms also tends to become larger. Therefore, when we are multiplying the number of these groups, we are actually doing something about conversion.

Concerned Fellowship

We have been talking about the *importance* of fellowship in the foregoing paragraphs. But now let us hasten to say that fellowship for its own sake should not be a goal. There are grades of fellowship which do not represent all that we mean by "Christian fellowship." Unfortunately, even church groups sometimes develop a type of fellowship which is so limited and restricted that it becomes selfish. These kinds of groups hinder evangelism and the cause of Chirst because they:

• develop into "cliques,"
• become "mutual admiration societies,"
• resemble social clubs which completely fail to express Christ's concern for others.

Such "closed corporations" are not in harmony with the mind of Christ and may do the church more harm than good.

Every church school class must have an evangelistic concern if it is to be Christian. This will express itself in a

- desire and conscious effort to extend the fellowship by discovering and attracting new members,
- glad willingness to accept new people into the fellowship of the group.

The class that is motivated by a Christian concern will reach out to all people.

At its best, every church school class above the young children's departments will be a fellowship of learners who are concerned about reaching the unreached and surrounding them with the redemptive love of Christ. This concern will grow as the

- teacher portrays appealingly the redemptive love of God in Christ.
- students experience the reality of God and dedicate themselves to his purposes.
- students take part in activities through which they develop and express their interest in the needs of others.

Making Fellowship Calls

In an earlier chapter we discussed the importance of making fellowship calls. In order to secure the best results when calling on prospective members, callers should be coached in advance to:

- indicate what the church has to offer,
- describe the character of the program,
- tell something about the persons who make up the class membership,
- explain a little about the study materials that are used.

It will be helpful if the caller can take along a printed or mimeographed leaflet or prospectus which describes the entire program of the church school and related groups. When the call is made on a child, it may be well to take along one of the take-home reading books to leave in the home.

Try to arrange for a definite time—possibly "next week"—when the prospect will attend. The caller might offer to accompany the person if he or she hesitates going alone into an unfamiliar situation.

Finally, some counsel for the callers would be to:

- Remember the purpose of every visit.
- Prepare mentally and spiritually.
- Know how to interest others in the call.
- Know how to introduce yourself.
- Be alert for additional information to be passed along to the pastor and the church school superintendent.
- Record all important facts of the call before they are forgotten but *not* until you leave the home.
- Emphasize the friendly welcome that will be awaiting the new member at the church school.

For Thought and Discussion

1. How important is fellowship to a program of evangelism in the church school?

2. Is fellowship in the church school always concerned fellowship? What is the difference between fellowship for its own sake and Christian fellowship?

3. What counsel would you give to persons who would make fellowship calls?

I AM THE VINE

YOU ARE

THE BRANCHES

5 Affirming Our Roots

Highlighting the Central Elements of Our Faith

In the achievement of its purposes, the church school uses certain resources which are generally not available to secular—public school—education, namely,

> the basic elements of the Christian faith revealed through the Word of God, the Bible.

The elements with which church school teachers will have to deal are the

- tragedy of sin,
- grace of God,
- redemptive love of God in Jesus,
- recreative power of the Holy Spirit,
- coming of the kingdom of God,
- new persons in Jesus Christ.

Church school leaders should never lose sight of these basic elements of our faith. They constitute the task peculiar to the church school as contrasted with that of the public school.

The teachers of children must recognize that these elements are mature concepts. The theological ideas developed in this chapter are not intended to be used as teaching material in the children's departments, but

teachers of children need to have a faith based on
these elements.

This chapter only *highlights* the basic elements of the Christian faith and is written for mature teachers and leaders to explore further in order to

develop their thinking, their faith, their lives.

The elements are assumptions of the Christian faith which should be central in every teacher's and leader's experiences. Persons for whom these theological assumptions have little meaning will find it difficult to fulfill their evangelistic responsibility as church school teachers or leaders. We will list them here and comment briefly on each assumption with the hope that you will be

motivated to pursue further study in order to have a
better understanding of the faith you want to
impart to others.

Sin—What Is It?

Christian faith says that each of us—though made in the image of God—is a sinner. The human problem is not simply that we do certain things we ought not to do. (See Romans 7:14-25.) The whole bent and direction of our lives are the problems.

Sin is

- more than a series of moral failures;
- a person's revolt against God;
- a person's desire to claim a greater place in the scheme of things, at any cost;
- self-centeredness, egocentricity.

The above statements lead to the conclusion that "all have sinned and fall short of the glory of God" (Romans 3:23). (See also Romans 5:12-21; Galatians 3:22.)

This is a universal fact of human experience. No person escapes this involvement in sin.

So serious is this involvement in sin that we cannot remove ourselves from it by our own efforts. Our salvation is ultimately dependent upon God's grace. Our deliverance from sin is not our achievement; it is God's action through Christ.

The final word of Christian faith is not in despair of humanity; it is an affirmation of confidence in God:

> "Where sin abounded, grace did much more abound" (Romans 5:20, KJV).

The Grace of God

As we said in an earlier paragraph, we have been created in the image of God. Because of this fact we have the potential of becoming his "special" children. There is a bent to goodness implanted within each human soul in spite of the reality that we are born with sinfulness as one of our commonest characteristics. It is inevitable, then, that our bent for sin and our desire for goodness should come into conflict and create a state of tension.

Well, what was God to do with sinful humanity—those who were to be his children, created in his own image—when they turned from his way and chose instead the ways of evil and destruction?

Our Bible is the story of

God's redemptive acts, the history of God's grace.

And finally in the fullness of time, God sent his own Son into the world. Through Jesus Christ, the love of God, free and unpurchased, comes to bless humanity with forgiveness and salvation. He is the supreme revelation of God's grace.

Through Christ

> "we have obtained access to this grace in which we stand, and we rejoice in our hope of sharing the glory of God" (Romans 5:2).

The Redemptive Love of God in Jesus

The "gospel" or "Good News," then, is the story of God's redemptive love as it has been revealed to us through Jesus Christ. His work here on earth must be regarded as a unit. Of course, for our purposes, it is helpful to divide his time on earth into several parts. In our teaching we often deal with small bits, such as an incident, a parable, or a single statement. However, it is important for students above primary age to see the work of Christ as a whole and for its major elements to stand out clearly.

A brief summary of these elements would include:

The Incarnation

In a unique and mysterious way, God entered into the world through his Son, Jesus Christ, and thus revealed himself to humanity, "that God was in Christ reconciling the world to himself" (2 Corinthians 5:19, NEB). Someone put it this way, "Jesus is God, spelling himself out in language we, as humans, can understand."

The Life of Jesus

Our knowledge concerning the life of Jesus is derived chiefly from the Four Gospels. The three Gospels of Matthew, Mark, and Luke include a narrative account of the life of Christ which follows the same outline and includes material common to all three.

The Gospel of John, although containing some biographical material, is more interpretive.

All Four Gospels describe
- the ministry of Jesus,
- the healing and teaching activities of Jesus,
- the miraculous deeds of Jesus,
- the principal events leading to the death of Jesus.

Jesus' Teachings

The teachings of Jesus are consistent with both the
- Old Testament law and the
- New Testament moral code.

The early church did not differentiate the ethical teachings of Jesus from the gospel.

Ethical teachings make up a large percentage of the recorded words of Jesus. Eliminate the ethical content of the Sermon on the Mount, the parables, and the informal discourses of Jesus; then eliminate the ethical content of the writings of Paul, and you will greatly reduce the length of the New Testament. It is obvious that Jesus expected his teachings to be taken seriously:

"Why do you call me 'Lord, Lord,'
and not do what I tell you?" (Luke 6:46)
and
"Go therefore and make disciples of all nations"
(Matthew 28:19*a*).

The Death of Christ

To be sure, the teachings of Jesus are set forth in some detail in the Gospels. However, the incidents leading up to the crucifixion occupy even a greater place in those writings. The Four Gospels contain a total of eighty-nine chapters, and thirty-one of these have to do with the closing events of Jesus' life. Obviously the Gospel writers considered the crucifixion to be an experience of profound significance. The writings of the apostle Paul reinforce this estimate with many statements similar to 1 Corinthians 1:18:

"For the word of the cross is
folly to those who are perishing,
but to us who are being
saved it is the power of God."

Related to the crucifixion is the Christian doctrine of the *atonement*—that through Christ's death on the cross, sinful human beings are given the possibility of reconciliation and fellowship with God. Many theories of the atonement have been written, and yet not one of them can fully explain this great mystery. The significance of Christ's vicarious death on the cross is greater than any theory and beyond the power of mortals to describe fully.

The Resurrection

A well-known painting by Eugene Burnand portrays the disciples on the day following the crucifixion. They have returned to the upper room where last they had had fellowship with the Master. Judas, of course, is missing. The picture, known as *Holy Saturday,* shows the disciples utterly despondent, dejected, and defeated. Their great Teacher and Friend, whom they had believed to be God's Messiah, was crucified and buried. All the hopes he had kindled in their hearts were gone. And yet, these same frustrated men would soon be going out to overcome the pagan world with courage and victory.

How do we account for this radical transformation? It is not explainable except for the *resurrection* and the experience of the living Christ in their lives. Having been assured that Christ was raised from the dead, they could say with Paul:

"Neither death, nor life, nor angels, nor princi-
palities, nor things present, nor things to come, nor
powers, nor height, nor depth, nor anything else in

all creation, will be able to separate us from the love of God in Christ Jesus our Lord" (Romans 8:38-39).

"And with great power gave the apostles witness of the resurrection of the Lord Jesus, and great grace was upon them all" (Acts 4:33, KJV).

The Holy Spirit

In his disclosure at the Last Supper, Jesus told his disciples that after he went away, he would send to them "the Counselor." Following his resurrection, Jesus again foretold the coming of the Spirit:

"But you shall receive power when the Holy Spirit
has come upon you; and you shall be my witnesses
in Jerusalem and in all Judea and Samaria and to
the end of the earth" (Acts 1:8).

This prediction was fulfilled on the day of Pentecost when the disciples were gathered together in Jerusalem,

The New Testament teaches that the functions of the Holy Spirit are to
- convince people of sin (John 16:8),
- guide them into truth (John 16:13),
- initiate the new birth (John 3:5),
- transmit the love of God (Romans 5:5),
- produce the fruit—"love, joy, peace, patience,
kindness, goodness, faithfulness, gentleness, and
self-control" (Galatians 5:22).

The Kingdom of God

After his baptism and temptation, Jesus began his ministry of teaching and preaching. In his very first message as recorded in Mark, he stated that "The time is fulfilled, and the kingdom of God is at hand . . ." (Mark 1:15). Teaching about the kingdom and helping people meet the requirements for membership seem to have been his major concerns.

As we read the Gospels, we realize that the kingdom has a present and a future aspect. It is here now: "The kingdom of God is in the midst of you" (Luke 17:21). But it also is to come in the future. (See Matthew 19:28; 26:29.) It is therefore apparent that we are to live in the kingdom now and meet its requirements, but that sometime in the future the kingdom will be ushered in with a completeness that is not attainable now.

Some of the basic ideas that Jesus taught about the kingdom are that it

- is entered as one becomes like a little child (Mark 10:14-15),
- comes as we do the will of God (Matthew 6:10),
- is capable of growth and development (Matthew 13:31-33),
- is of the greatest value (Matthew 13:44, 45),
- is to be sought above all else (Matthew 6:33).

The church should be thought of as one of the mediums through which persons enter the kingdom and learn to participate in its life.

The New Person in Jesus Christ

The becoming of a human being into a child of God, a "new person in Jesus Christ," is the emphasis of the mission of the Christian church. To work with God in effecting this change is the basic purpose of Christian education. Therefore, every session, every program, every experience in the church school must be in some way related to this purpose, or it becomes irrelevant and inconsequential. The process by which one becomes a "new person in Jesus Christ" is two-fold; it is a process in which

God has a part and
we have a part.

God's Part

The word which theologians have used to describe God's part is

"regeneration,"

the process by which a person is "born again," in which God bestows new life.

Regeneration is the loving and gracious act of God which brings a person into a relationship with his or her heavenly Father so that one becomes "a child of God." This new union produces a change of character, a moral change. The person becomes, as Paul says,

"a new creation"

and is empowered by the Holy Spirit to live on a new level of righteousness and love and service.

Our Part

Conversion is the human counterpart of regeneration. It is our acceptance of God's forgiveness and grace. We change from one attitude or condition to another. It involves the acceptance of a new and better standard. Through Christ a new way and a new life have come into view.

According to the New Testament, faith in Christ is at the heart of the conversion experience: "But to all who received him, who believed in his name, he gave power to become the children of God" (John 1:12).

Faith in Christ is

- an acceptance of him as mediator of God's grace and redemptive love;
- a response of the individual to the whole work of Christ—
  -his unique and divine character,
  -his life and teachings,
  -his atoning death on the cross,
  -his resurrection;
- an admission of Christ to the center of one's life and a surrender of one's will to him.

For Thought and Discussion

1. What are the basic elements of the Christian faith?

2. Plan a series of sessions with the pastor or some other person knowledgeable in theology who can discuss the elements of the Christian faith with you.

3. Ask the pastor or some other staff member to recommend a book or books to help you gain a better understanding of the elements of the Christian faith.

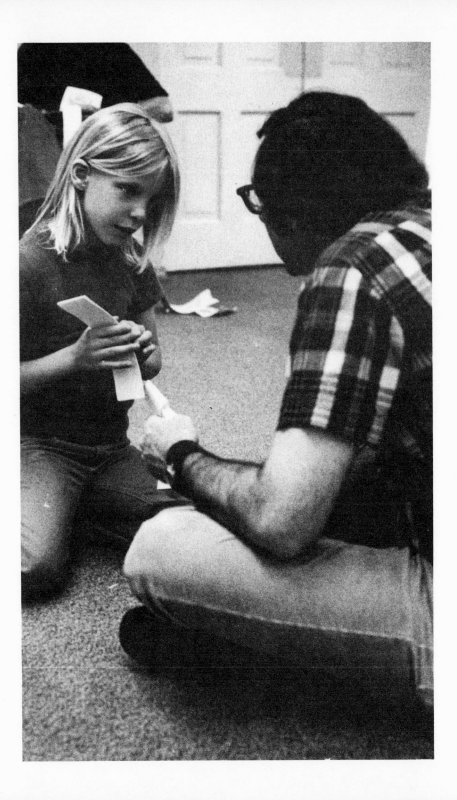

6 Teaching for a Decision

In the preceding chapter we discussed the "central elements" or theological presuppositions which underlie the church's program of evangelism. These are the basic convictions that constitute the gospel message.

The Process of Becoming a Christian

Now let us consider a possible process by which one becomes a Christian, viewing the role of the teacher in the process. We may suggest a logical progression, such as

- acquaintance,
- appreciation,
- commitment,
- reorganization.

Acquaintance and appreciation are preparatory in their natures and look forward to the experience of commitment. Commitment, of course, is a major element in the conversion experience and is the focal point of evangelism. Reorganization is an expected outcome of commitment and naturally follows it.

What, then, is involved in this suggested process of evangelism?

Let's begin with

Acquaintance

A person must first gain an acquaintance with God's revelation in the Bible, particularly with Jesus Christ.

The church school has a concern for providing this kind of information. Since God has graded children, teaching also must be graded. "Milk for babes," admonished Paul. So a selection of truth which will have meaning within the child's experience must be made. Gradually the child gains a knowledge of Christ and His significance.

Even older classes in the church school should provide students with the kind of study content that will develop acquaintance with Christ and lead to the experience of conversion. This presupposes that these classes will have in their membership some evangelized persons—which indeed they will have if they are performing the function of a recruiting agency.

Appreciation

To become a Christian, a person must not only have an acquaintance with Christ, but he or she must also have an appreciation of Him and His significance. The individual must respond to Christ with trust, love, and dedication.

While appreciation must always have an intellectual content, it lies particularly in the realm of feeling. Feeling, or emotion, is exceedingly important in religious development. It gives to religion the sense of reality and significance. It is the mainspring of motivation. Vital religion must be an affair of the heart as well as the mind.

Naming "appreciation" as the second stage does not imply that it necessarily follows the first stage in point of time. Acquaintance and appreciation can happen simultaneously—and usually do. As we learn about Jesus, our appreciation of him is likely to grow.

So it is with the church school teacher. The teacher can present factual knowledge about Jesus. But unless the teacher can transfer to students his or her own appreciation and enthusiasm for Christ, he or she has failed at the most important point. To be sure, the teacher's faith cannot be transferred. But that faith can be exposed in such a way that the students can appropriate it for themselves.

Commitment

God has endowed us with the power to make our own choices.

The kinds of decisions we make determine the quality of our lives. We begin making decisions in early childhood. Even a young child is faced with choices—bad or good, better or best. As they are given Christian standards for decisions and are guided in making right choices, they learn to commit their way to the Lord from early childhood.

All of these experiences involving choice are preparations for the day when a person is to make the great choice, a commitment to Christ, a decision to accept him as Lord and Savior.

- *ACQUAINTANCE* with Christ is primarily an intellectual experience.
- *APPRECIATION* of Christ involves the emotions.
- *COMMITMENT* is an appeal to the will, a volitional experience. It is a response of the entire personality— intellect, emotion, and will—to the person of Christ, a complete surrender of the will to God.

While stressing the significance of early conversion, we would not wish to suggest that *special* effort be made to secure decisions from younger junior children or children in the Primary Department. They are very impressionable, and it is easy for adults to pressure these younger children into making decisions before they are ready for a vital and meaningful experience. This results in an injustice to the child, to the church, and to the Holy Spirit. Many young children have a pseudoexperience of conversion which may prevent them from experiencing the real thing. On the other hand, let's not minimize the securing of commitments from older children!

Let us press with vigor our program of winning for Christ high school youth and adults. Many ex-students whom the church school has lost have gone through the first two stages in the process of evangelism; they have become *acquainted* with Christ, and they have developed varying degrees of *appreciation* of him. But they have become detached from the church before the church school has helped them to the third stage—*commitment.*

Many churches have organized an effective program through which teams of lay persons visit unchurched people in the community and invite them to make a Christian commitment or to attend the church. Many of the persons reached by such a program have at one time attended church school where they had learned about Christ. The great success of home visitation programs dramatizes the failure of the church school to carry its students through *all* the stages of educational evangelism, including the third, *commitment,* and the fourth,

Reorganization

When a person decides to be a Christian, included in the decision is the commitment to place Christ at the center of his or her life and to reorganize that life around Christ. The person has previously given Christ a place in his or her life; now Christ is given the preeminent place—the center—of that life. The person says, with Paul, "This one thing I do. . . ." "For me to live is Christ. . . ." "That in all things he might have the preeminence."

Culbert G. Rutenber, in *The Price and the Prize,* refers to this experience as the time of inward renewal

> when by surrender and commitment to him the Christ of history becomes the internal Christ. The personality of Jesus then links itself redemptively to the personality of the believer, and these two become one. . . . To ask a man to follow Jesus or to obey his teachings is merely to drive him to despair. But if Jesus Christ could become the Guest of his soul and live his life all over again through his body, things would be different. And Christian faith insists that Jesus Christ can do just that![3]

The Teacher's Responsibility

What is the church school teacher's responsibility in each of the above stages through which a person becomes a Christian?

The teacher has responsibility in all the stages discussed in this chapter. All the stages are important, but it is the third one, commitment, which is central to the teaching program: to become a new person in Jesus Christ. As we stated in an earlier chapter, the materials and methods should seek to lead to the experience of conversion.

Making a commitment in connection with a personal interview is preferable to a decision made within the class or department program.

There is great temptation for children and junior highs to "follow the leader," and they may respond to an invitation in imitation of others without fully understanding the meaning of what they are doing.

[3]Culbert G. Rutenber, *The Price and the Prize; an Interpretation of the Christian Gospel for Young People* (Valley Forge: Judson Press, 1953), pp. 97-99.

In a personal interview, the teacher can make sure that the student understands the implications of the decision and is expressing his or her own deep desire.

Interviewing Older Juniors and Junior Highs

The teacher who is concerned about the spiritual growth of students will

- arrange for a private interview with each boy or girl.
- make careful preparation for the interview:
  - rethink all he or she knows about the child—needs, interests, problems;
  - talk with the child's parents first;
  - pray for wisdom and understanding for both herself or himself and the student.
- arrange for the interview to be in a place where conversation will be private and uninterrupted.
- approach the subject simply and directly:
  - express satisfaction and joy in evidences of the student's spiritual growth.
  - "I wonder if you have come to the time when you would like to take your stand publicly as a follower of Jesus and join the church?"
- discover—if the student expresses interest—how clearly the step taken is understood.
- determine what further help and explanation are necessary.

Interviewing Older Youth

During the period of middle and later adolescence, most persons make three important choices in life:

- the choice of a lifework,
- the decision about marriage,
- the determination and crystallization of a philosophy of life.

This age is surely the age of crisis. Making the wrong choice in any of these three areas can be traumatic—sometimes affecting the rest of one's life. How imperative that we reach young people for Christ at the earliest possible opportunity, so that their choices will be influenced by their faith in him!

A further reason for urgency in the evangelizing of youth is that adolescence represents the period in which we lose the majority of our students from the church school and many of them from the church. The church has a legitimate concern to win these young people for Christ and keep them in the life of the church.

Young people will respond naturally to the appeal to Christ:

- Christ's courage and self-sacrifice wins their loyalty.
- They appreciate his idealism, for they, too, are idealists.
- They have a strong sense of need as they face new problems and make the transition from dependence to independence.
- They want a satisfying life for themselves and want to make a contribution in making this a better world.
- They need the help of Christ.

Interviewing Adults

With some adult classes, it may not be possible for a teacher to visit every prospect.

Such classes should have a visitation committee which is trained in the techniques of evangelistic calling. The teacher and visitation committee select the names of those who are not professing Christians and then develop a definite plan of visiting them and discussing their relationships to Christ.

There are available, denominationally and interdenominationally, definite programs for interviewing prospects in home visitation evangelism.

For Thought and Discussion

1. What are the logical stages of progression in becoming a Christian?

2. What is the teacher's responsibility in helping the student to achieve the suggested stages in conversion?

3. How would the teacher go about preparing to interview older juniors or junior highs to discuss their readiness for a commitment to Jesus Christ as Lord and Savior of their lives?

4. What should be kept in mind when interviewing youth?

5. Who should visit adults, and how would one go about interviewing them?

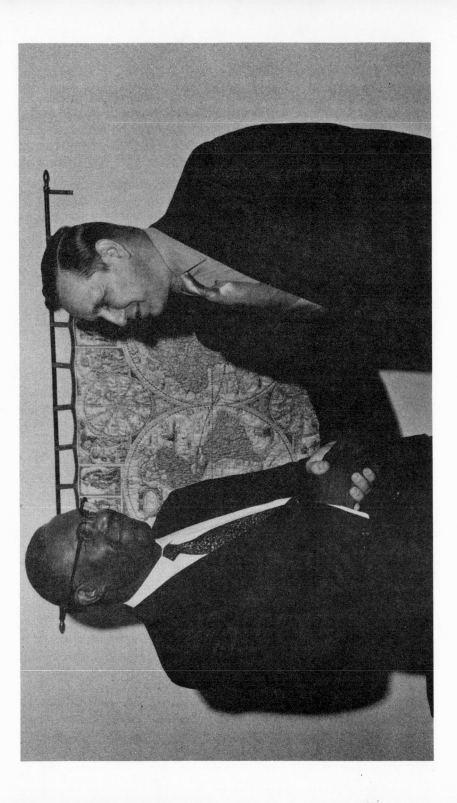

7 Building Persons into the Life and Ministry of the Church

Joining the Church

Conversion marks the beginning of a new life! But it is not the end of our responsibility to the convert. The church must nurture the new life and offer every possible assistance that will help the new Christian grow in grace. The first step will be to

bring the convert into the life of the church

and all that this relationship implies.

We must make a clear distinction between the act of conversion and the act of joining the church. Conversion is not primarily a commitment to join the church, rather it is a commitment to Christ as Lord and Savior. Joining the church is secondary, although it follows almost inevitably. Care must be taken that unregenerate persons are not invited to join the church with the same casualness with which a person is invited to join a fraternal order or a parent-teacher-student association or the Boy or Girl Scout troop.

The church is different from all other organizations.

The church is the Body of Christ!

It is composed of believers who have made the great commitment of their lives to Christ. They have chosen him as the center of their motivation. Once the commitment has been made and the convert begins to organize his or her life around Christ, becoming a part of the fellowship of believers will follow naturally.

Discipleship and Church Membership

A person who joins the church must have an understanding of

- its nature—what it is;
- its function—what it does;
- his or her responsibilities—what is expected.

Churches provide this kind of instruction in special

discipleship and church membership classes.

Junior and junior high curricula usually carry units of study on the meaning of church membership. But it is essential to conduct additional classes for all age groups.

While the invitation to join discipleship and church membership classes is usually extended to everyone, the classes are intended particularly for those who are planning immediately to join the church. Some churches make attendance in such a class a requisite for joining the church.

Some churches—especially larger ones—often schedule several series of discipleship and church membership classes throughout the year. They usually culminate just before Christmas, Easter, Pentecost Sunday, or some other significant time in the church year. This type of year-round program avoids giving the wrong impression, voiced by a student, "Is Easter the only time a person can join the church?"

The church school in which teachers have a vital concern for the evangelistic goal to lead persons to the experience of conversion will maintain the kind of spiritual climate in which the Holy Spirit exercises his regenerative power often throughout the year. This results in conversions and the need for holding discipleship and church membership classes frequently.

Reception into the Church

It will help us to understand the significance of this occasion if we put ourselves in the place of the new member and that person's new relationship with the church. The new member is to be received officially and welcomed into the community of believers as the pastor extends the hand of fellowship. Then the new member will enter into that mystic communion which Christians share with Christ and with one another as they fellowship around the table of our Lord.

The church school teacher should be one of the first to greet the new member at the close of the Communion service and express joy that the student is now officially a part of the church fellowship.

Many churches have a procedure of assigning a sponsor to "watch over" each new member. Whether or not such a plan is used, the church school teacher should serve unofficially as the sponsor of new church members from her or his church school class.

The teacher will encourage the new member to

- attend church worship services regularly,
- engage in personal, daily devotions,
- practice the principles of stewardship,
- enter increasingly into the fellowship and work of the church.

The sponsor can have a more natural and helpful relationship with the new member by inviting him or her home for an evening meal and get-acquainted visit.

In addition to extending the hand of fellowship on a Sunday morning, many churches have a public reception for new members. Following a brief program, there is often a reception line for new members and refreshments are served.

Church school teachers should always be present at such occasions to help their students get acquainted and feel at home.

Involving Members in the Church's Ministry

Elton Trueblood suggests that the word "member" and the biological term "membrane" come from the same Latin derivation and have a similar meaning. A membrane is a living tissue, a part of a living organism. It is alive, active, and it functions harmoniously with the other tissues which make up the organism. In somewhat the same way, church members are membranes in the body of Christ— the church. Each member must be spiritually alive and act in harmony with the other members if the church is to function successfully. This is simply a restatement of what the apostle Paul wrote to the Corinthians nineteen hundred years ago:

"Now you are the body of Christ and individually members of it" (1 Corinthians 12:27).

When persons join the church, we have a responsibility to build them into its life and ministry and help them become living membranes of the body of Christ.

The ministry of the church was given to the entire church; hence every member of the church is responsible for its ministry. We must help every new convert find some opportunity for service in the life of the church—and find it early. The church is a training ground for ministry, and it must help each member to be a servant in the world within the context of his or her opportunities—his or her own maturity and abilities, relationships, and involvements in the world.

In *The Church's Teaching Ministry,* Kenneth L. Cober says,

> If we believe that the ministry was given to the whole church, then every member becomes responsible for its ministry. . . . The time-honored phrase, "the priesthood of all believers," should be restated in our day as "the ministry of all believers." When a person joins the church he becomes a member-minister. . . . Christ incorporates us into the full life of his church and its ministry. To become a church member means to respond to the call of Christ, to become united with him in his death and resurrection, to identify one's self with God's mission, and to participate in the life of the church and its ministry in the world.[4]

The Perfecting of the Saints

The "divine-human" encounter which results in conversion is not the ultimate goal of Christian life—only the beginning. God has never fully revealed himself at any one time. His revelation in the Bible extended over a period of more than a thousand years. God does not say everything that he wants to say to a person at the time of conversion. In the act of regeneration, the Holy Spirit makes of the convert a new person but does not make of that person all that he or she ought to become. New Christians are still "babes in Christ" and must grow into Christian maturity. The Christian will *continually* say with the apostle Paul, "Not that I . . . am already perfect . . . I press on toward the goal." (See Philippians 3:12, 14.)

The church school teacher has the opportunity of helping the new Christian reorganize his or her life around Christ. Taking one's place in the church is only a part of this reorganization. Now that Christ has been made the Lord of the person's life, the new convert will examine his or her conduct and motives to see if they conform to his or her Christian profession:

[4]Kenneth L. Cober, *The Church's Teaching Ministry* (Valley Forge: Judson Press, 1964), p. 37.

- What practices, patterns of conduct, need to be changed?
- What spiritual disciplines should be established?
- What new activities ought to be undertaken?
- What attitudes need to be Christianized?

As new horizons unfold and new sights into God's purposes are revealed, the Holy Spirit will move again to waken the conscience and demand further obedience of the growing Christian. These new promptings of the Spirit will lead to a deepening of the spiritual life and a desire to establish Christian relationships within the community, the nation, the world.

Through the

- unfolding of Bible truth,
- understanding of Christian truth,
- application of Christian truth,
- personal interest and concern of the teacher,
- fellowship with other Christians,
- development of devotional practices,
- and many other ways,

the church school class

will help its members grow in the grace and truth of Jesus Christ.

Next to the joy of leading a student to know Christ as Lord and Savior, is

the teacher's satisfaction of sharing in the divine-human process through which the students grow more and more like the Master.

"Go therefore and make disciples of all nations, baptizing them in the name of the Father and of the Son and of the Holy Spirit, teaching them to observe all that I have commanded you; and lo, I am with you always, to the close of the age."
(Matthew 28:19-20)

For Thought and Discussion

1. Is "conversion" the same as "joining the church"? What's the difference?

2. What must a person understand about the church before he or she becomes a member?

3. What part should the teacher take when a student is received into the church?

4. What do we mean by "the perfecting of the saints"?

Suggested Bibliography

General Educational Planning

Blazier, Kenneth D., and Huber, Evelyn M., *Planning Christian Education in Your Church.* Valley Forge: Judson Press, 1974. A guide with step-by-step suggestions for the board or committee of Christian education for planning the overall program of the year. Also in Spanish: *Planificando la Educacion Christiana en Su Iglesia.*

Cober, Kenneth L., *Shaping the Church's Educational Ministry: A Manual for the Board of Christian Education.* Valley Forge: Judson Press, 1971. Handbook for a church's board or committee of Christian education. A discussion of a philosophy, structure, and planning for Christian education in a church. Also in Spanish: *Mejorando el Ministerio Educativo de la Iglesia: Un manual para las Juntas de Educación Cristiana.*

Church School Planning

Blazier, Kenneth D., *Building an Effective Church School: Guide for the Superintendent and Board of Christian Education.* Valley Forge: Judson Press, 1976. Handbook for superintendents and boards or committees of Christian education. Considers purpose, standards, expectations, and organization for the church school as well as job descriptions for workers, planning for the year, and motivating leaders.

Blazier, Kenneth D., *A Growing Church School.* Valley Forge: Judson Press, 1978. Suggestions for helping church schools grow in both numbers and quality.

Blazier, Kenneth D., and Hanson, Joseph John, *Launching the Church School Year.* Valley Forge: Judson Press, 1972. Suggestions for many aspects of the school year: recruitment, orientation of leaders, enrollment, visitation, teacher support, training of leaders, Launch Sunday.

Cully, Iris V., *New Life for Your Sunday School.* New York: Hawthorn Books, Inc., 1976. A guide to making the most of the church school. Helpful for superintendents and boards or committees of Christian education.

Leader Development

Huber, Evelyn M., *Enlist, Train, Support Church Leaders.* Valley Forge: Judson Press, 1975. Practical guide for a church's board or committee of Christian education, nominating committee, and other boards.

Turner, Nathan W., *Effective Leadership in Small Groups.* Valley Forge: Judson Press, 1977. For leaders of classes, church boards, and committees. Deals with the stages of development experienced by most groups, leadership styles, and creative use of conflict. Outlines five local church workshops to train group leaders.

Ministry with Children

Isham, Linda, *On Behalf of Children.* Valley Forge: Judson Press, 1975. A consideration of the needs, development, and abilities of children, and suggestions for developing objectives and plans for ministry with children.

Ministry with Youth

Carroll, John L., and Ignatius, Keith L., *Youth Ministry: Sunday, Monday, and Every Day.* Valley Forge: Judson Press, 1972.

Help in planning for ministry with youth: philosophy, programming to respond to needs, selection and training of leaders, and organization.

Evans, David M., *Shaping the Church's Ministry with Youth*. Valley Forge: Judson Press, 1977. A revised edition of a popular book calling for a reappraisal of ministry with youth in a church.

Ministry with Adults

Leypoldt, Martha M., *Learning Is Change*. Valley Forge: Judson Press, 1971. Although written primarily for teachers of adults, this book will also help administrators understand adults—who they are and how they learn—as well as give other insights helpful in planning for ministry with adults.

Ryan, Roy H., *Educational Ministry with Adults*. Nashville: Discipleship Resources, Board of Discipleship, United Methodist Church, 1972. A planning guide for persons responsible for ministry with adults. Consideration of philosophy, designing settings and groupings, organization, selection of resources, and training leaders.